Romney,
Hythe &
Dymchurch
Railway

IN COLOUR

Derek Smith

IAN ALLAN
Publishing

First published 1993

ISBN 0 7110 2192 9

Published by Ian Allan Ltd, Shepperton, Surrey; and printed by Ian Allan Printing Ltd, Coombelands House, Addlestone, Surrey KT15 1HY.

Previous page:
Green Goddess passes between the old and the new *en route* to Dungeness Lighthouse in August 1990. *J. B. Snell*

Right:
Green Goddess with a down train from Hythe to Dungeness about to cross the Willop Bridge in June 1955. This bridge was unusual in that it was formed in the shape of a steel trough, in which the track was laid amid several tons of ballast. It was condemned in 1968 and rebuilt in the more usual open girder style in the following year. The coaches are an interesting mix of pre and postwar vehicles, including several 1934 'Hudson-Hythe' saloons, a 1954 Hooper-built 'Queen Anne' and the 1904-vintage Heywood closed coach from the Duke of Westminster's Eaton Hall Railway. *J. B. Snell*

Introduction

The 15in gauge Romney, Hythe & Dymchurch Railway opened between New Romney and Hythe in 1927. The following year an extension beyond New Romney to Dungeness brought the total length to 13.5 miles. The railway was financed by Capt J. E. P. Howey, a wealthy miniature railway enthusiast who employed the respected engineer Henry Greenly to design virtually everything required to build a one-third full-size main line railway.

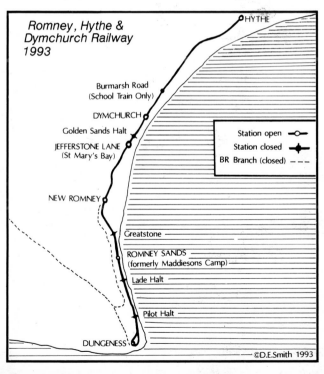

Romney, Hythe & Dymchurch Railway 1993

- HYTHE
- Burmarsh Road (School Train Only)
- DYMCHURCH
- Golden Sands Halt
- JEFFERSTONE LANE (St Mary's Bay)
- NEW ROMNEY
- Greatstone
- ROMNEY SANDS (formerly Maddiesons Camp)
- Lade Halt
- Pilot Halt
- DUNGENESS

Station open ○—
Station closed ●—
BR Branch (closed) – – –

©D.E.Smith 1993

For many years the locomotives of the RH&DR only came in two colours — London & North Eastern Railway green, or black. In the late 1930s Capt Howey, who had already had his favourite engine *Hurricane* fitted with a non-standard tender of a new and larger design, decided to paint the locomotive blue. How far, and in which direction this prewar customising of individual locomotives would have gone if more pressing international matters had not intervened, we shall never know.

When peace returned in 1945 and the railway was returned to the Captain further changes had already been made to the locomotives by the Army, and this policy of livery changing and subtle restyling has continued ever since.

To chart pictorially all of the postwar changes to the fleet of locomotives would need a much larger book than this. If we added all of the changes to rolling stock, station layouts, buildings and lineside scenery then we would no doubt require as many volumes as a well-known encyclopaedia. So what I have tried to do within the confines of this book is to show just a few of the changes that have taken place to both the moving and static parts of the railway since 1955, a date of no greater significance than it happens to be that of the oldest colour slide that I have included.

Deciding which photographs to use and which to discard has been a nerve-wracking process. There will always be gaps in any published work but I hope that the contents of the following pages will, if nothing more, add some visual substance to fond memories.

Derek Smith

New Romney, Kent
January 1993

Front Cover:
Southern Maid seen just after leaving Hythe on the new deviation. This was opened in 1990 to enable the adjacent Hythe Engineering site to be redeveloped. *P. H. Groom*

Back cover:
Doctor Syn leaving New Romney bound for Hythe. *J. B. Snell*

Acknowledgements

In compiling this book I have been fortunate in being able to draw upon the memories of several people who have given up their time, information and picture collections quite freely. George Barlow, John Snell and Tony Crowhurst have contributed the bulk of the earlier material, while the more modern collections of Peter Groom, Euslin Bruce and A. F. Porter have filled in the gaps. Over the last few months most of the staff have become accustomed to being asked rather strange questions about various aspects of the railway, but I think that Richard Batten, Fred Sargent, Ray Holyer and Andy Mullen deserve particular thanks for patience beyond the call of duty.

Finally I would like to thank Harry Smith who first introduced me to the joys of the Romney in 1954. These days he spends most of his time during Special Events in the Heywood Buffet up to his elbows in washing-up water, but fortunately he still manages to get out and take a few pictures — thanks Dad.

Left:
Seven years later, this August 1962 photograph shows *Green Goddess* stopped at the down home signal outside New Romney. Although a number of the coaches still date from before the war, the whole train has a much more 'cared for' look than in the previous picture. As with all of the British outline locomotives *Green Goddess* started life with the standard Greenly-designed small tender. During the 1946/47 rebuild at the Southern Railway's Ashford Works the small tender was discarded in favour of a new larger high-capacity one. *J. B. Snell*

Right:
By the time this picture was taken in August 1967 Capt Howey had died and his widow had sold the railway to two retired bankers. Outwardly all seems calm and secure as an immaculate *Green Goddess* stands on the turntable at Hythe. Behind the scenes mounting repair bills for essential work on bridges, rolling stock and track were giving considerable cause for concern. *J. B. Snell*

Left:
In 1981 *Green Goddess* surrendered her large tender to *Northern Chief* and was sent to TMA Engineering in Birmingham for a major overhaul. When the engine returned to New Romney it was complete with a brand-new tender built to the railway's own design. In September 1985 the *Goddess* took part in the Old Oak Common Depot open day, where visitors had a perfect opportunity to compare the merits of both broad and minimum gauge locomotives side by side. *P. H. Groom*

Right:
In 1989 it was decided to reunite *Green Goddess* with her old high-capacity tender and it is in this form that she is shown here in winter snows at the Warren. Although the railway now has two powerful diesels for use out of season, at least two steam engines are kept serviceable during the winter for use on Santa Specials or private charters. *D. E. Smith*

Left:
Although all of the locomotives were originally built with parallel lagging, several of them, including *Northern Chief*, have acquired a taper effect. Unlike most of the other locomotives, the *Chief* kept her original tender during the postwar rebuild. This excellent picture was taken in the mid-1970s and shows *Northern Chief* crossing the New Cut near Botolphs Bridge Road.
A. R. W. Crowhurst

Right:
In 1974 a new passing loop was installed adjacent to Maddiesons Holiday Camp. This gave a passing place on the single track between New Romney and Dungeness and considerably eased train operation over this section. In this picture the driver of Dungeness-bound *Green Goddess* exchanges the single-line tokens with his opposite number on *Northern Chief. J. B. Snell*

Left:
Following an overhaul at TMA in 1981 *Northern Chief* lost her small tender to *Hercules* and received the large capacity tender from *Green Goddess*. In this picture *Northern Chief* is seen on the turntable at Hythe while working on the 1988 Santa Specials. The state of the motion and wheels has been caused by wet rust on the rails, fortunately the steel work is protected by thick grease, but it is still going to be a long job to get the underneath into the immaculate state normally expected of a Romney engine. *P. H. Groom*

Right:
In 1989 *Northern Chief* and *Green Goddess* exchanged tenders. Following this No 2 received a complete repaint in a green livery similar to that used by British Railways in the 1950s. In August 1990 *Northern Chief* is seen crossing the New Cut bridge between Hythe and Dymchurch. *Euslin Bruce*

Above:

During the war the Army gave *Southern Maid* a coat of 'Wickham blue'. In the 1947 rebuild at New Romney the locomotive reverted to green and the *Maid* received a new high-capacity tender built at Ashford Works. In 1954 the engine appeared in a new umber livery similar to that once used by the London, Brighton & South Coast Railway and it is in this state that she waits at Hythe with the down 'Marshlander'. *G. A. Barlow*

Left:

In 1959 *Southern Maid* underwent another change of livery, this time to French grey — a colour that did not photograph well in overcast weather! This photograph of Hythe with *Southern Maid* being prepared to work the down 'Marshlander' contains a wealth of interesting features, especially with *Typhoon* waiting to leave with a crowded train from platform No 4. *RH&DR*

Right:

By the time this picture was taken in 1976 *Southern Maid* had acquired a fully-lined Great Northern green livery. The train is crossing Hoornes Sewer between Bumarsh Road and Dymchurch with a rake of brown and cream coaches. Over the years the railway has experimented with several different liveries for the coaching stock and the return to the earlier brown and cream colour scheme took place in the 1970s. In 1983 this gave way to the current red and cream scheme. *A. R. W. Crowhurst*

Left:
Having spent many years away from the railway, some of them as part of a scrap heap in Belfast, *The Bug* finally returned to active service on the RH&DR in 1977. Rescued by Sir William McAlpine and restored to former glory by Dick Cushing and his son in Kent, *The Bug* is seen here in steam at New Romney just after her return. In the background a row of the 1929 12-seater Clayton Pullmans are being broken up. *J. B. Snell*

Below left:
In 1984 several Romney locomotives and coaches were leased out for use at the Liverpool Garden Festival. Although *The Bug* proved powerful enough to move the required length of trains it was too slow to keep up with the intensive pace of operation of the railway, so it saw little service. Here it makes a rare sortie out onto the main line as it pilots fellow RH&DR loco. *Black Prince. J. B. Snell*

Right:
Since 1977 *The Bug* has seen considerable service, especially at Christmas when it takes on the mantle of Father Christmas's sleigh during the Santa Specials. In 1991 the engine underwent a comprehensive overhaul as can be seen from this picture taken in the erecting shop at New Romney. During the overhaul the locomotive received a new 'improved engine green' livery based on that designed for the London, Brighton & South Coast Railway. *D. E. Smith*

Left:
The Bug is pictured in early 1992 with a mixed train at Half Mile Curve. The wagon directly behind the engine is used by the engineering department as a re-railing equipment store. Appropriately enough it has the fleet number '999'. Over the past few years the railway has attracted a number of sponsors for some of its rolling stock, including Kodak, Courage and Eastbourne Buses. *D. E. Smith*

Right:
In 1940 *Hercules* was converted by the Army to form part of a miniature armoured train. The conversion involved fitting the locomotive with some fairly heavy armour plating and putting her between two converted hopper wagons. Fire-power consisted initially of two Boys Anti-Tank rifles and four elderly Lewis guns. The latter were eventually replaced with Brens. To commemorate the 50th Anniversary of the Battle of Britain in 1990 a replica suit of (plywood) armour was made up for *Hercules*. Working from old photographs one of the armoured wagons was also recreated. The Armoured Train is seen standing in the siding at Dymchurch station during the Military Railway Day in September 1990. *Harry Smith*

Left:
In 1946 *Hercules* became the first RH&DR locomotive to be overhauled at the Southern Railway's Ashford Works. During the overhaul the opportunity was taken to replace the original Greenly-designed tender with one of the new high-capacity types. An unfortunate error in measurement meant that the new tender was too high in proportion to the rest of the locomotive. Although the cab roof was raised to counteract the discrepancy *Hercules* remained an ugly duckling until the tender was rebuilt in 1959. With the tender problem cured the engine emerged from the works in a 'Midland lake'-type livery. She is seen here in the early 1960s leaving Hythe. *G. A. Barlow*

Right:
One of the joys of travelling on the Romney, Hythe & Dymchurch is the chance that you might pass a train travelling in the opposite direction. In this picture the driver of *Green Goddess* has captured the moment as he crosses with *Hercules* near Golden Sands. In the background the wood and asbestos chalets typify the holiday camps that thrived in the area up until the package tour boom of the late 1960s. Although the chalets were replaced by more comfortable caravans in the 1970s the camp closed at the end of the 1989 season. *G. A. Barlow*

Left:
In 1952 Walt Disney paid a visit to the RH&DR and rode on *Green Goddess*. Twenty years later, in 1972, the railway provided *Hercules* and a special train to take some of his better-known characters to Maddiesons Camp. By this time the Midland lake had been replaced by a much brighter red known as 'Dahlia'.
A. R. W. Crowhurst

Right:
In 1978 *Hercules* was sent to Dick Cushing for an overhaul. Unfortunately Dick died before the work was completed and the overhaul was eventually finished at New Romney. Following the overhaul *Hercules* inherited *Northern Chief's* small Greenly tender and a new livery similar to the dark red used by the Metropolitan Railway. In 1986 *Hercules* and regular driver Derek Walsh visited the Ravenglass & Eskdale Railway in Cumbria, and in this picture they are seen leaving Ravenglass with a train of very mixed R&ER rolling stock.
J. B. Snell

Left:
Because of derailment problems encountered with the long fixed
wheelbases of the two 'Mountain' class 4-8-2s neither *Hercules* nor
Samson saw much service before the war. By 1939 *Samson* had been
stripped of all useful items and could be seen lying derelict in New
Romney yard. Fortunately most of the small radius points that had
caused the derailment problems had been replaced by the time the war
ended and it was decided to send *Samson* for rebuilding at Clifford
Edwards of Hove in readiness for the expanding ballast traffic. In
1955 the postwar Malachite green livery was exchanged for a lined
black scheme similar to that used by the London & North Western
Railway. This picture shows *Samson* in August 1962 about to pass
under Littlestone Road and into New Romney station. The second
coach is of interest as this is *Martello*, one of the two observation cars
built just after the war to run as part of the crack 'Bluecoaster Lim-
ited'. Above the concrete wall, on the right, a Hastings diesel unit can
just be seen standing in the platform of the Southern Region's New
Romney station. *J. B. Snell*

Right:
Following an overhaul in 1974 *Samson* was briefly fitted with some
spare smoke deflectors that had come from *Southern Maid*. The original suggestion to fit deflectors to a Romney engine came from driver
Bob Hobbs when he proposed fitting some to *Green Goddess* in 1950.
In the end they were fitted to *Hurricane* and over the next few years
several other locomotives were similarly modified. The temporary
attachment of the spare smoke deflectors to *Samson* was only sup-
posed to last for a few days, but in the end they remained in place for
several months. *A. R. W. Crowhurst*

Left:
Due to the varying water conditions on the Romney Marsh, the RH&DR has always suffered with a build-up of scale in the locomotive boilers. In the past the only way to counteract this problem was to add a chemical treatment to the water and ensure that each boiler was washed out thoroughly after every four or five days of use. To try to improve matters a proper water treatment plant has recently been installed at New Romney so that all water columns are fed with the correctly treated water. A programme of fitting every locomotive with a blow-down valve is also underway and here we see the driver of *Samson* blowing the engine down on the turntable at New Romney. The valve is fitted in the lowest part of the boiler and, when opened, a mixture of high pressure steam and water blows out the solid particles that have collected, thus stopping the formation of scale. *J. B. Snell*

Left:

Typhoon was the first of the two powerful three-cylinder Pacifics built by Davey Paxman. Due to maintenance difficulties with the third cylinder and inside valve-gear it was converted to the standard two-cylinder design in 1935. At the same time her appearance was slightly altered by the fitting of tapered lagging sheets. In keeping with most of the other British-style locomotives *Typhoon* received a new high-capacity tender shortly after the war. In this picture, dating from the late 1950s, the driver of *Typhoon* awaits the right of way from the Station Master at Dymchurch. The fashions of the young audience contain almost as much variety as the set of coaches that will soon be on their way to Hythe. *RH&DR*

Left:
In May 1964 *Typhoon* completes an attractive picture as she enters Hythe. Directly behind the engine is the brake van built by Sir Arthur Heywood in 1896 for the Duke of Westminster's Eaton Hall Railway. This came to the RH&DR in 1947 when Capt Howey purchased the remains of the railway from the Duke's estate. The locomotive waiting to depart is *Winston Churchill*. *J. B. Snell*

Right:
The engineering department at New Romney is split either side of the main line. On the down side is the locomotive shed and machine shop, while on the up side is the erecting shop which contains a large roof-mounted crane capable of lifting a locomotive boiler from its chassis. Being divided in this way is not the most convenient working arrangement but I am sure that this point is the last thing on the mind of the driver of *Typhoon* as he heads the last train of the day from New Romney to Hythe into the setting sun. *J. B. Snell*

Left:
In 1988 *Typhoon* was overhauled at New Romney. At the same time it was decided to repaint the engine in the olive green of the Southern Railway. This picture, taken in August 1990, shows the locomotive emerging from the down side portal of the Prince of Wales bridge. Greenly's original concrete structure was perfect for the era in which it was built, but with the ever-growing residential developments in the Palmarsh area the low parapets were bound eventually to cause a problem. To counteract this a more substantial wall was built on top of the original. This modification may have improved safety, but it certainly did nothing for the bridge's looks! *J. B. Snell*

Right:
The long evening shadows and setting sun give little clue to *Hurricane's* true colours as she makes her way under Littlestone Road bound for Dungeness in June 1955. To the left of the picture can be seen the level crossing that carried the standard gauge siding from British Railways' New Romney station into the RH&DR property *J. B. Snell*

Left:
Taken looking south, this 1962 picture shows *Hurricane* about to enter the Littlestone Road tunnel, while *Green Goddess* stands on the old down road. Above them both a standard tank can be seen arriving at New Romney (BR).
G. A. Barlow

Right:
Following a repaint in 1987 *Hurricane* appeared in a lighter blue than in previous years and was completed with a white cab roof. The first job for the locomotive was to haul the 'Hobb's Choice' special, which was run in honour of ex-driver Bob Hobbs. The train is seen on the down run just south of Romney Sands. Although the whitewashed coal was only provided for this one trip, the cab roof remained white until repainted into the more standard black the following year. *J. B. Snell*

This fine view of *Hurricane* on Hythe turntable was taken in the early 1970s. As the second of the two three-cylinder Pacifics *Hurricane* was Capt Howey's favourite engine. In 1934 he broke with tradition and had a new large-capacity tender constructed to replace the original standard design. It was modelled on the corridor tenders in use with the London & North Eastern Railway and was complete down to the fitting of a dummy corridor connection. In 1937 the valve gear that connected the centre cylinder to the rest of the motion tied itself in knots out in the middle of the Marsh. The loco was towed back to New Romney in disgrace and was hastily converted to two-cylinder operation. In 1938 *Hurricane* exchanged her standard green livery for one of Caledonian blue and was renamed *Bluebottle* — a name she was destined to keep until 1945. *RH&DR*

Left:
In 1962 *Winston Churchill* reverted to all black and received a new tender. The body of the tender was constructed by Gowers and it was mounted on the underframe of the tender from *Doctor Syn.* This late 1960s picture shows the locomotive entering New Romney with a down train while *Green Goddess* prepares to leave for Hythe. *RH&DR*

Right:
To give some idea of the relative costs between coal and oil operation *Winston Churchill* was fitted with oil burning equipment in 1972. In 1973 she was sent for overhaul to Wingham Engineering, near Canterbury, returning in 1974 sporting a rather bright red livery, as seen here at Dymchurch in 1976. The oil burning trial lasted until 1979, but no significant savings were noted. *A. R. W. Crowhurst*

Left:
In 1990 *Winston Churchill* was one of the engines leased to the Bure Valley Railway. The BVR is a 15in gauge line constructed on the trackbed of an abandoned standard gauge line from Wroxham to Aylsham. During its stay in Norfolk the engine enjoyed several mishaps, including being derailed and rolling onto its side. The locomotive is pictured here in happier times entering the loop at Coltishall *en route* to Aylsham. *P. H. Groom*

Right:
In 1991 the engine returned to the Romney Marsh and, following some heavy repairs to the motion and axle-boxes, it re-entered service later the same year. It is seen here on 8 September 1991 leaving Hythe with a non-stop shuttle bound for New Romney. The darker 'LMS red' livery and lettering was applied during an overhaul prior to the visit to Norfolk. *Euslin Bruce*

Left:
This interesting view of Dungeness was taken in the late 1950s before the new lighthouse was built. In the station *Green Goddess* stands ready to work the up 'Marshlander' while the driver of *Dr Syn* oils round. In 1953 *Dr Syn* had received one of the strangest liveries applied to a Romney engine — Great Western green with maroon wheels and yellow lining! *G. A. Barlow*

Above right:
During her 1964 overhaul *Dr Syn* received a new tender similar to the one built for *Winston Churchill*, she also received an all over black livery. In this picture, taken shortly after her return to service, *Dr Syn* and 'The Blue Train' get admiring glances from passengers at New Romney. *G. A. Barlow*

Right:
In 1976 *Dr Syn* made the long journey north to the Ravenglass & Eskdale Railway, where she is seen crossing with *Northern Rock* at Irton Road. Seeing a picture like this makes one wonder how the Ravenglass & Eskdale would have developed if Capt Howey had been successful in buying the line in 1924. *J. B. Snell*

Left:

In 1986 it was decided to give *Dr Syn* a more authentic American profile by raising both domes and extending the chimney. To finish the job a permanent headlight was mounted in front of the new copper-capped chimney. Although the steam locomotives are normally only used on passenger services, they do occasionally turn up as part of a strange working. In this shot, taken during the 1992 Steam & Diesel Gala Day, *Dr Syn* is seen between Greatstone and Romney Sands with a mixed freight and passenger train. The two yellow vehicles in the centre of the train are the platelayers' tool truck and the mess coach, the latter being one of the only two heated coaches on the railway. *Euslin Bruce*

Right:

In 1976 the RH&DR acquired a second-hand steam locomotive from Germany. on arrival in Britain the engine was found to be in remarkably sound condition and, apart from a repaint and alterations to allow the driver to sit with his head below the level of the cab roof, very little work needed to be done before it entered service. The engine, number 11 in the Romney fleet, received the name *Black Prince* which had lain unused since the renaming of the original *Black Prince* to *Doctor Syn* in 1949. *A. R. W. Crowhurst*

Left:
It is difficult to believe that only a few months separate this picture from the previous one. *Black Prince* was one of three locomotives built by Krupps of Essen (Germany) in 1937. The other two locomotives had already arrived in Britain when news came through that the third was still available. Arrangements were made for shipment and the locomotive is seen en route to the Romney Marsh. *J. B. Snell*

Below left:
In 1980 *Rosenkavalier*, one of the other two Krupps locomotives, made the trip from Norfolk to Kent and is seen double-heading with *Black Prince* at the Warren. One of the problems with visiting locomotives is that very few are compatible with the RH&DR's vacuum brake system, so they are unable to operate service trains without a Romney locomotive in attendance. Although this can be a nuisance, it does result in some interesting double-headers. *J. B. Snell*

Right:
Although based on the Romney Marsh *Black Prince* has become a well-travelled engine with trips to Ravenglass, Liverpool, Japan and Norfolk over the last few years. In 1984 the locomotive was in service at the International Garden Festival in Liverpool where it is seen threading its way between the many flower beds that bordered this popular but short-lived line. *J. B. Snell*

Left:
In 1989 it was decided to make several modifications to *Black Prince* to allow for easier maintenance. At the same time several cosmetic changes were made, including the replacement of the old smoke deflectors with smaller 'bat wing' types. In May 1991 the locomotive makes an interesting comparison with *Northern Chief* as they double-head an up train away from Dymchurch. *J. B. Snell*

Right:
Following trials with *Shelagh of Eskdale* from the Ravenglass & Eskdale Railway, the RH&DR commissioned their own diesel from TMA Engineering of Birmingham. Designed for use on the schools' contract service and in general passenger service, the diesel was delivered to New Romney in 1983. Because of its association with the school contract the engine was given the name *John Southland*, after the man who gave the original local education bequest in 1610. *John Southland* is seen outside New Romney shed shortly after delivery together with *Shelagh of Eskdale* and *Winston Churchill*.
A. R. W. Crowhurst

Left:
In 1989 the RH&DR took delivery of its second diesel. Outwardly similar to *John Southland* the new engine contained several refinements considered necessary after experience gained with its predecessor. The livery, which is based on that used by the Union Pacific Railroad, was applied as a tribute to the late Earl of Lindsay, Chairman of the RH&DR until his death in 1989, who had spent some years working on the Union Pacific. *J. B. Snell*

Right:
One important role of the diesels is with the permanent way gang. Although the railway has various small internal combustion-engined locomotives, including a Simplex, they offer very little protection for the driver from both the weather and the possibility of a collision on a level crossing. Whenever possible all permanent way operations and track patrols are now carried out using either *John Southland* or *Number Fourteen. D. E. Smith*

Left:
As already mentioned the railway owns several small internal combustion engines, including this Simplex. It was the only locomotive acquired by Capt Howey when he purchased the stock of the Eaton Hall Railway in 1947. Initially the only modification made was to cut the cab down to enable it to operate safely within the RH&DR's reduced loading gauge, but in later years various changes were made to the engine, including the conversion of the locomotive from petrol to diesel operation. It is seen here in 1972 about to pass under the Warren Bridge with the annual weedkilling train. *J. B. Snell*

Right:
By the time this photograph was taken in 1990 the diesel-mechanical drive of the Simplex had been replaced by a diesel-hydraulic unit and the locomotive now had the luxury of an electric start. This special mixed train was run as part of the 1990 Steam & Diesel Gala and is seen just south of Britannia Points heading for Dungeness. *Euslin Bruce*

Left:
Since *Sutton Flyer* became the first 'foreigner' to visit the Romney in 1959 many locomotives have made their way down to the Romney Marsh. Some have come in the name of research, while others have been brought down purely for the pleasure of running them on the longest stretch of 15in gauge railway in the world. In 1979 the scale *Flying Scotsman* made an interesting comparison against *Samson* at New Romney. *J. B. Snell*

Right:
Some visitors stayed longer at the Romney than others as could be witnessed in 1979 when most of the rolling stock that Captain Howey had purchased from the Eaton Hall Railway just after the war was returned to the care of the Duke of Westminster. It is planned that the vehicles will eventually be restored to original condition and be placed on display at Eaton Hall. *J. B. Snell*

Left:
During the trials designed to formulate ideas for the proposed new diesel engine the RH&DR benefited from visits by both *Shelagh of Eskdale* and *Lady Wakefield* of the Ravenglass & Eskdale Railway. The latter locomotive was always going to be a tight fit through the tunnel under Littlestone Road but it wasn't realised how tight until the tunnel forcefully removed the roof-mounted air horns. Fortunately no other serious damage was done and with the air horns now mounted on the bonnet *Lady Wakefield* soon proved a very useful locomotive during its 1980 visit. *J. B. Snell*

Right:
In 1985 the RH&DR celebrated the 60th anniversary of *Green Goddess* and *Northern Chief*, both of which had been built by Davey Paxman of Colchester. Altogether the Essex firm was responsible for seven of the Romney engines so to complete the celebration it was decided to invite the Ravenglass & Eskdale Railway to send their 1923 Davey Paxman-built engine, *River Esk*, to Romney. For the first time all the railway engines built by Davey Paxman were gathered together and several 'Paxman Jubilee' special trains were run, this one being a double-header with *River Esk* and *Southern Maid. D. E. Smith*

Although *Winston Churchill* was once displayed in a Toronto department store, no Romney locomotive has so far made it to the USA. It therefore seems ironic that in the space of four years the RH&DR should have been visited by two locomotives from the same railway in California. The first to visit was *Fern* a 4-4-0 narrow gauge type locomotive and this was followed in 1992 by the 4-6-0 *Sequoia*. Both locomotives came from the Redwood Valley Railway and proved very popular with both visitors and staff alike. *Fern* is seen on the turntable at Hythe, while *Sequoia* becomes the topic of conversation at New Romney. *J. B. Snell/Euslin Bruce*

Right:
The locomotive that seems to have stirred more memories than most visited the railway in May 1992. Originally built in 1909 by Bassett-Lowke for the Franco-British Exhibition *Red Dragon* had spent many years operating under the guise of *Prince Edward of Wales* on the Dreamland Miniature Railway in Margate. Having spent many years derelict and in pieces, the engine was purchased by the owners of the Lakeside Miniature Railway in Southport, who commissioned Austin Moss to rebuild it. The visit to Romney caused a considerable amount of local interest, with lots of people remembering riding behind it at Margate — or in some cases actually having driven it. *Red Dragon* is seen here being prepared outside the erecting shop at New Romney in May 1992.
Euslin Bruce

Left:
In 1950 Capt Howey purchased a full-size 0-4-4T named *Dunrobin* from the estate of the Duke of Sutherland. It was duly delivered to New Romney complete with a rather ornate private carriage and was stored in an old Nissen hut at the end of the standard gauge siding. Once or twice each summer the engine would be steamed up and down the short siding for the benefit of both staff and visitors. When Capt Howey died in 1963 *Dunrobin* was sold, along with everything else, to Messrs Collins and Scratcherd. As the engine and coach earned little or no money for the railway, the new owners decided to sell them as quickly as possible. In the end, and much to the chagrin of the Sutherland family, the train was sold to an operator in British Columbia, Canada, where it remains to this day.

Although it was a sad loss, it is worth pondering upon the fact that a similar fate could have befallen the rest of the railway if it had not been for the effort and enthusiasm of those who have worked hard to keep the Romney, Hythe & Dymchurch Railway alive.
G. A. Barlow

Right:

Reckoned to be the oldest operating 15in gauge steam locomotive in the world *River Irt* made the long journey south from Ravenglass in 1991. Originally built by Sir Arthur Heywood as *Muriel* in 1894, the engine was rebuilt to a 'miniature' outline in 1927. In 1972 a more appropriate cab, dome and chimney were fitted to try and balance her appearance, and it was in this incarnation that she visited New Romney. Fortunately the limiting factor to operations of the RH&DR — the Littlestone Road tunnel — proved no obstacle to this fine locomotive, even though clearance was down to less than a quarter of an inch. *J. B. Snell*

Epilogue

Inset:

As if to prove that locomotive livery changes are a continuing theme at the RH&DR, a deal has been arranged between the railway and Eastbourne Buses that un-named diesel No 14 will operate in the bus company's colours during 1993. The repainting, which is to celebrate Eastbourne Buses 90 years of operation (thus making them the oldest municipal bus operator in the world), was undertaken at the Birch Road depot and workshops where No 14 is seen alongside some unusual shed mates.
Derek Smith